DATE ABUSE

Herma Silverstein

—Issues in Focus—

ENSLOW PUBLISHERS, INC.

Bloy St. & Ramsey Ave. P.O. Box 38
Box 777 Aldershot
Hillside, NJ 07205 Hants GU12 6BP
U.S.A. U.K.

Library of Congress Cataloging-In-Publication Data

Silverstein, Herma.
    Date abuse / Herma Silverstein.
       p. cm. — (Issues in focus)
    Includes bibliographical references and index.
    ISBN 0-89490-474-4
      1. Dating violence—United States—Juvenile literature.
[1. Dating violence.] I. Title. II. Series: Issues in focus
(Hillside, N.J.)
HQ801.83.S55 1994
306.73—dc20   93-25011
                                      CIP
                                        AC

Printed in the United States of America

10 9 8 7 6 5 4 3 2 1

Cover Illustration: © Stuart Simons, 1993

Contents

To everyone who has suffered the pain and humiliation of date abuse, with the hope that this book might help in some way.

Preface

This book is meant to "inform teenagers about the current problem of teen date abuse" only.

The mention of date rape is discussed only as *one* symptom of date abuse, *not* the foremost or the only symptom. This book does not mean to imply that all teenagers who date have sex, nor that all teenagers in an abusive dating relationship get raped.

Further, although there is mention of date abuse situations in which one of the partners has been murdered by the other partner, this too is only *one* symptom of date abuse, and a rare, extreme one at that.

The author and editors want to make it clear that this book is not meant to frighten, or to imply that all dating situations end in abuse. In fact, most teenagers who date or go steady do not experience abusive relationships. But there *is* a growing number of date abuse cases, and this book is written to talk about them, in order to help teenagers who are involved in abusive dating situations find ways to get out of them, and also to help teenagers who are *not* involved in date abuse avoid becoming involved in abusive dating relationships.

1

Date Abuse: What Is It?

Sitting on the couch in her basement rec room, Jennifer, 16, tried to force the tears back into her eyes as she watched the couples laughing and dancing to the music. New Year's Eve was supposed to be so romantic, and she'd spent days planning this party with her two best friends. Everything had turned out perfectly—decorations, food, CDs.

What wasn't perfect was Rob. After all the months they'd been dating, why didn't he know she loved only him? If she wanted to dance with someone else, it was just because Rob didn't like to dance, and she did. What was wrong with being friends with other guys? It was no big deal. Why couldn't Rob kick back like the other guys? Why did he have to get so jealous over nothing?

Now it was almost midnight, and while everyone else would be kissing in the new year, she'd be stuck on the couch alone while Rob sat in a corner giving her the silent treatment. The silent treatment wouldn't be so bad if Jennifer didn't know what would come next. Once the other couples left and they were alone, Rob would get nasty. He'd call her names and shove her around. Probably hit her. Jennifer's friends were always telling her to break up with him. But Rob said if she left him he'd get even and really hurt her.

Across town, on this same New Year's Eve, Scott, 17, started to pull into his driveway, then suddenly drove on down the street. His old girlfriend, Tyla, was standing in his driveway, waiting for him again.

Why doesn't she stop stalking me? Scott thought. I've told her a million times we're through. If she doesn't stop phoning me all the time, I'll go crazy. I can't even go out of my house anymore without her following me. She even follows me on my dates. That girl's so obsessed, who knows what she'll do next?

Tyla, meanwhile, had seen Scott drive past his house. She had been waiting for him for five hours, and she would wait five more hours if that's what it took to get to talk to him. Tyla just *had* to talk to Scott. If he'd only listen to her for one second, she knew they'd get back together.

Even though Scott broke up with her two months ago, Tyla couldn't stand being without him. She wrote him letters, left notes on his door, and phoned him at least twice a day, just to hear his voice. Once she got so mad she slashed his tires. She'd begged Scott to go back with her, but he said he loved Melissa now. Tyla even tried to ruin Melissa's reputation by spreading false rumors about her. But Scott didn't believe anything Tyla said.

As the night wore on, Tyla became more and more desperate. If Scott didn't come home soon, she'd just knock on his door and ask his parents to let her wait for him inside. And if they wouldn't, she'd do something even more terrible to Scott than slashing his tires—she'd do *anything* to get him back.

Jennifer and Scott, living on different sides of town, are both in date abuse situations. And their experiences are not at all uncommon. Date abuse is a rising crime in the United States. Statistics show that as many as one-third of all high school and college-age students experience date abuse in some form.

What Exactly is Date Abuse?

Date abuse is any hurtful or unwanted behavior done to another person by a dating partner. Date abuse can be physical, verbal, emotional, or sexual. *Both boys and girls can be date abusers.*

Physical Date Abuse

Physical date abuse is any bodily contact that hurts the other person, including hitting, punching, shoving, grabbing, beating, kicking, biting, choking, throwing things, pulling hair, and using a weapon against another person. Physical abuse does not have to leave a mark. It only has to be hurtful or unwanted. *Hurtful* or *Unwanted.* These are the key words to knowing if you have been abused by your date.

For example, you might ask yourself some questions. Did your date ever shove you in anger, dig fingers into your skin when grabbing you, or "playfully" slap you? Are there bruises where your date punched you in the arm? Is it hard to talk about something your date did, even if it happened a long time ago? Answering yes to any of these questions means that you have experienced physical abuse.

Some forms of physical abuse are hard to recognize. Playfully wrestling with a date, for instance, is not abuse. But if the wrestling gets rough and you get hurt in any way, such as having your arm twisted or your leg bruised, the "play" has gone from a *wanted* act to an *unwanted* act, and from playing to abuse. Further, if you tell your date to stop and he or she won't, you are being abused. Any act that begins as joking around but ends in pain is abuse. The key idea here is that your date did not stop the behavior when you asked.

Physical abuse may leave serious, permanent injuries, such as loss of hearing from a hit on the head; broken ribs from being kicked; kidney failure from a beating on the back; or loss of sight from a punch in the eye.

Sometimes, physical abuse can become so violent that it ends in death. Thirty percent of female murder victims in the United States are killed by their husbands or boyfriends. And 20 percent of these women are between the ages of 15 and 24. The following are frightening stories, but they are examples of what has happened to *some* teenagers.

Stacey McLaughlin, 17, from Chicago, was strangled by her boyfriend two weeks before her high school graduation. The reason? He did not want her to go to college where she would meet other boys.

Michelle Hartfield, 17, of Minnesota, hitchhiked with her boyfriend, Curtis Smith, a 24-year-old construction worker, to a motel in Springfield, Missouri, on a job search. When they failed to find work, Michelle wanted to stop looking and go home. But Curtis tried to make her stay. When she refused, they got into a violent argument. And in a fit of rage, Curtis shot Michelle in the head.

When Jennifer Crompton, 14, tried to break up with her overly possessive boyfriend, Mark Smith, he stalked her for several months, even breaking into her home and stealing things from her room. Finally, he stabbed her to death in her own home.

Verbal Date Abuse

Verbal date abuse in a dating relationship involves put-downs, swearing, belittling comments, threats, shouting, name-calling, or any other hurtful or unwanted verbal outbursts, such as yelling, "Get over here, you stupid idiot!" "Who else but me would want you?" "I don't know why I waste my time with you." "Who was that guy/girl you were talking to?" "Why weren't you home when I phoned?"

Often verbal abuse happens when one dating partner feels emotionally or intellectually threatened by a self-confident partner with high self-esteem.

This is what happened to a sixteen-year-old girl who tried to tell a boy she had dated only a few times that she didn't want to see him anymore. He went into a rage, screaming, "Who do you think you are? I've picked up better-looking chicks off the garbage heap. You'll be lucky to find a retard to take you out, you're so disgusting."

Everyone sometimes has arguments with the person they date. But for some couples, verbal abuse takes up practically the whole relationship. When this happens, it is a sign that the abuser needs to control the other partner.

Emotional Date Abuse

Emotional date abuse is any behavior that leaves the other person feeling hurt inside. Often emotional abuse is a *lack* of behavior, such as ignoring or not talking to the other person, promising to do something and not following through, breaking dates at the last minute, standing up a date, or withholding attention and affection.

Emotional abuse is the hardest type of dating abuse to recognize because you cannot actually *see* the scars it leaves. For example, you are dating someone who breaks dates all the time. There is nothing you can point to and say, "Look at how you hurt me." The wounds are inside, where only you can feel them.

Sexual Date Abuse

Sexual date abuse is any bodily contact that is unwanted or hurtful—from hugging, kissing, or touching, to forced intercourse. Even holding hands can be sexual abuse if one person does not want to hold hands and the other person forces them to.

Studies show that one-fourth of college women either experience attempted rape or are raped. And 90 percent of the victims know their rapist. Men can be victims of rape as well.

Forced sex is still rape even if the couple have been dating a long time or have had intercourse previously. Any previous consent to sex does not automatically mean consent on later dates. This misunderstanding is why many victims fail to report the crime. They do not think they have been raped, since on an earlier occasion, they had intercourse with their partner.

Sexual abuse can occur from force, threats, trickery, or pressure. To identify sexually abusive behavior, you might consider these questions: Do you want to be involved in sexual behavior right now? Are you having sex because you want to or because

14

your date wants you to? Are you frightened or intimidated by your date? Often you may not want to do something, but you do not want to hurt your date's feelings, or you are frightened of your date, so you give in rather than say no.

Why Does Date Abuse Happen?

Professional counselors say the main reasons are jealousy and anger. These emotions often come from old-fashioned expectations about what is "proper boy and girl behavior."

Until the women's liberation movement of the late 1960s, it was traditionally believed that the boy was the dominant, macho half of the relationship. He was responsible for asking the girl out, deciding where to go and with what other friends, coming to the girl's house to pick her up, paying for the date, and starting any sexual advances such as kissing, touching, or intercourse.

If the relationship continued, it was also up to the boy to ask the girl to marry him. The girl would never suggest marriage out loud, even though she might think about marriage constantly.

These false behavior roles for males and females are still going on. For many teenagers, aggressive and hurtful behaviors are not considered abuse, but rather standard operating procedure in the dating game.

However, the false separation of male and female dating roles can be abusive. The boy always comes first—so the girl is not an equal partner in the relationship. The boy is boss—and has the right to say how the relationship works.

This attitude makes the girl a willing slave to the boy's wishes. If the girl has friends who are dating each other but who are not also friends of the boy's, the girl's friends are not asked to double-date.

The boy, expecting to be the one giving the orders, can easily fall into abusive behavior if his orders are not obeyed. If he decides they are going to a certain movie, but the girl does not want to see that movie, he may insist they go. If he decides they are going to a party at the house of someone whom the girl does not like, he may force her to go. Once there, if she does not do what he wants, he may yell at her or slap her around.

The girl, expected to be the quiet, shy partner, the one whose job it is to please the boy, goes along with whatever the boy wants, giving up her outside activities, friendships, and talents in order to give the boy her full attention. She even dresses and wears her hair in ways that please him. She puts up with his less hurtful abuse in order to avoid being more severely abused.

Failure To Tell

Too often the person experiencing date abuse never tells anyone and does nothing to stop it. Sometimes failure to tell is because the person feels there is no one to talk to about the abuse. Adolescence is a time of striving for independence from parents and developing a sense of who you are as an individual. Conflicts with parents over rules and behavior are common at this time.

Frequently, teenagers feel such a gap between themselves and their parents that they refuse to ask them for help in dealing with abuse in their dating relationships. They may fear their parents will either not believe them, or minimize the abuse by characterizing it as merely the overreaction typical of a teenager. Or they may feel ashamed to admit that someone has sexually abused them, because they mistakenly believe the sexual abuse was their fault.

This parent/teenager gap also encourages teenagers to seek out friends of their own age who understand and support them. Thus, having a boyfriend or girlfriend who is totally focused on them seems to supply the attention, love, and security the young person feels are missing at home. Often the person being abused may be frightened to tell anyone about it for fear the abuser will get angry and hurt them even more.

Fear of Being Different

Besides false male/female behaviors, another false idea that leads to date abuse is the belief that being normal means having a boyfriend or girlfriend. The fear of being different and not fitting in keeps many teenagers in violent relationships. They believe it is better to have an abusive boyfriend or girlfriend than not to have a boyfriend or girlfriend at all.

To stop date abuse, you first have to recognize that you are being abused. Then it is important to know why abuse happens, so you can prevent it from happening to you. To do this, you need to know what kinds of people abuse others, and what kinds of people allow themselves to be abused.

2

Who Are the Date Abusers and Why Do They Do It?

On our first date I told her I wasn't the type to go steady. But she said I was the only person she wanted to date. It killed her to see me with another girl. She started driving by my house all the time. If I was outside, she'd stop and talk to me for hours. I couldn't get her to leave. If I said I had to go, she'd start crying and beg me to "stay just one more minute." Finally I told her to leave me alone. The next thing I knew she'd gotten a butcher knife and slashed my tires. I guess she thought that way I couldn't go out with anyone.

—Brian, 17

He didn't threaten to hit me. He just hit me. It was so weird. He'd get this strange look, like a glare, or this real empty look, like he had nothing inside him. I knew bad things were gonna happen then. —Tanya, 14

I had to hit her. It was her fault I got so mad. She knew I didn't like her talking to other boys. So the only way to make her stop was to slap her around. After all, she was my girl. She belonged to me. —Mark, 16

After a while, I got scared to leave my boyfriend. I'd tell him I didn't want to go out with him anymore, and he'd slap me and say, "I'm not gonna quit till you tell me you're not leaving." —Beth, 15

One out of ten high school students has experienced physical violence from their dates. What causes a person to abuse a boyfriend or girlfriend? According to psychologists, these people believe life must suit them on *their* terms. They are the hub of the wheel; everybody else is a spoke.

Even in preschool, people with violent tendencies start showing this behavior. They bully others and purposely do what is forbidden. The child then expresses deep regret for his or her behavior, but later repeats the behavior.

As teenagers, abusers are usually poor students and may drop out of school. They deal with disappointment or rejection by becoming violent and irresponsible. They are likely to hit or beat a date in order to keep control of the relationship. If their dates do not go along with them, in their minds they have lost control of the situation. To abusers, that is like losing a part of themselves.

Mark Smith, who killed Jennifer Crompton, did not have a criminal record. But his mother testified that he had behavioral problems since the age of three.

While abusive boys tend to hurt their dates physically, abusive girls become violent in other ways. The girl destroys her boyfriend's personal possessions. Or she tries to ruin the reputation of any other girls he dates. She phones his house constantly, even late at night. Or she may follow him around and spy on him.

Here are some of the "whys" that go into the making of date abusers.

History of Living with Abuse

Experts find the abusive boy or girl often comes from a family in which physical violence and emotional abuse are used to express anger. They may have grown up seeing their parents drunk and settling arguments by breaking furniture, and hitting each other, or throwing things. These future date abusers learn that physical violence and other forms of abuse are accepted ways to handle their anger. And when older, they use abuse to deal with abuse in their dating relationships.

On the other hand, a person who comes from an abusive family learns that being abused is acceptable behavior from people who supposedly care about them, like their parents. They often do not even believe they are being abused. And when older, they expect abuse from their dating partners and therefore allow the abuse to continue.

Low Self-Esteem

Date abusers usually have low self-esteem. Being in control increases their self-esteem and allows them to get revenge for real or imagined wrongs. To stay in control, these teenagers use threats of violence or emotional harm against their dates. For example, if a girl has had sex with a boy, he may threaten to tell her family about it if she breaks up with him. Or a girl may threaten suicide in order to frighten her boyfriend into staying [not breaking up] with her.

By using threats, abusers may get their dates to do unwanted, hurtful, or illegal acts, such as stealing money from parents, shoplifting, or dealing drugs. Abusers then use their knowledge of these illegal activities to blackmail their victims into continuing the illegal activity.

Strong Male/Weak Female Role Models

Boys who believe the old cultural rule that men dominate women, and girls who believe that women are supposed to "stand by their man" at any cost, are likely to see physical abuse as acceptable behavior in order to keep the "strong male/weak female" role model in place. Such boys say they have a right to hurt their girlfriends if the girls do not do what they want. And the girls say they allow the abuse in order to please their boyfriends and to avoid further abuse.

Most abusive boys have the advantage of using their larger size to frighten their girlfriends into doing what they want. They make frightening gestures, smash things, use weapons, or drive dangerously. Abusive girls, on the other hand, usually frighten boys by withholding attention, affection, or sex.

Overly Possessive

People who are overly possessive can also be abusive dating partners. They have such little self-esteem and sense of their own identity that they cannot see where they stop and the other person begins. They view their boyfriend or girlfriend as an extension of themselves, as if they were Siamese twins. If their boyfriend or girlfriend breaks up with them, they experience the breakup as if they themselves had been killed.

These overly possessive date abusers spend most of their time spying on their partners. They phone them constantly to find out what they are doing. If the partner is not home when the abuser calls, the abuser may physically harm them. Eventually victims stay home "just in case he calls" in order to avoid further abuse.

The spying can be carried to extremes. One girl went to college in another state two thousand miles away to avoid her abusive boyfriend. He enrolled in the same college and switched his major to hers.

Isolating their dates from family and friends gives abusers more control. As a victim's friendships are broken, the victim becomes more emotionally dependent on the abuser. When the couple are constantly by themselves, instead of with other friends, it is easier for the abuser to use physical violence. For self-protection, the victim acts as the abuser wants, even when these acts are not in their best interests.

Emotionally Needy

Another type of abuser is emotionally needy. These people depend on their boyfriends or girlfriends to make them feel loved, wanted and secure. For such people, being with their boyfriends or girlfriends becomes a powerful craving. They confuse "I love you" with "I must have you."

Like drug addicts deprived of their drugs, they actually feel extreme pain when not close to the person they love. They believe they must see that other person right now; they cannot wait even a minute. Then if they phone their boyfriend or girlfriend, and the person is not home, the possessive date abuser becomes enraged, imagining the partner is out with someone else or has forgotten them. The possessive person says things like, "If you break up with me, I'll die," or, "If I can't have you, no one will."

Unsure Masculinity/Feminity

The obsessive boyfriend may be unsure of his masculinity and feel "like a sissy" when his girlfriend rejects him for someone else. This boy feels if another boy can date her, that boy is more of a man.

The obsessive girlfriend may be unsure of her femininity and feel unlovable and ugly when her boyfriend breaks up with her. She believes no one else will want to date her.

Refuses To Accept Responsibility For Behavior

Date abusers refuse to accept responsibility for their actions and instead blame their abuse on their victims. If the girl is not at home when he calls, even if she is just out with girlfriends, he believes she is picking up other guys, that she is deliberately doing this to be provocative or sexy.

In fairness, it must be mentioned that the way a girl dresses, speaks, and acts are messages as to how she wants to be thought of and treated. If a girl wears low-cut blouses, tight skirts, and heavy makeup, she might ask herself what message she is giving the boys she meets. Does this message imply she is a "party girl" and "easy"? Overflirtatious acts, such as leaning over a boy's shoulder while wearing a low cut T-shirt, will probably lead to the boy's "coming on" to her. This girl should ask herself whether this is the behavior she wants from the boy. If so, all well and good. But if not, she might consider how her dress and actions are attracting unwanted behavior from boys.

Abusive Dating Cycles

The obsessive relationship usually begins on an intense romantic note. He is Prince Charming. She is Cinderella. There is an almost too-good-to-be-true quality about the partner. The healthy partner is flattered for a while. They both think possessiveness means love.

But eventually the relationship becomes smothering. The healthy partner cannot even show a casual interest in someone of the opposite sex without the jealous partner flying into a rage. That is when the romance is over, and the arguments begin. Quarrels are quickly followed by emotional and physical abuse. Abusive partners tell their dates they deserve to be hit or hurt because they made them mad.

The abuser apologizes after the first slap or silent treatment, but then the cycle repeats and the abuse escalates. Now the abuser stops apologizing and blames the date for the violence. If unstopped, jealousy and anger grow stronger. The jealous partner eventually cannot tolerate the other person having anything to do with anyone else. Merely talking to friends of the opposite sex is seen as "cheating."

Now spying becomes the main obsession. Recently, the term "stalking" has come to mean this type of spying behavior. Stalkers are usually boys. They follow the girl everywhere, or get their friends to do so when they themselves cannot be around. The boy hides near the girl's house to check up on her, even coming by in the middle of the night and causing a scene. He phones at all hours to make sure she is home. If the girl breaks up with him, he makes threatening phone calls, writes abusive letters, and is physically abusive to her when he sees her in public. If not stopped, stalking can lead to more serious violence against the girl, sometimes even to murder.

The possessive girl, on the other hand, instead of stalking, tries to insert herself into the boy's life in every possible way. She phones him many times a day, and goes by his house constantly to see if he is home. Some girls even knock on the boy's door, demanding to see him. Or the girl tries to destroy the reputation of any other girl he dates.

Girls usually do not become physically abusive because the boy is usually bigger than they are. Instead, they often try to destroy the boy's possessions. For example, they may slash the boyfriend's tires, break his car windows, write abusive letters, or threaten to commit suicide if he breaks up with them.

Some Behaviors To Be Wary Of

If you feel that you might be in an abusive dating relationship, here are some behaviors to be wary of: Does your boyfriend or girlfriend phone to check up on you several times a day; seem to lack personal interests and goals; follow you around; discourage your outside interests and friendships; try to isolate you from your family and friends; make all decisions about what you will do and when; have preset ideas about your future, which you may not be in agreement with; refuse to settle differences with words, but show angry outbursts of temper instead; use violence that increases with the use of alcohol or drugs; or regularly ignore your opinion and values?

By thinking about these questions, you can become aware of behaviors that are abusive in dating relationships. You will be able to know before getting emotionally involved with a dating partner whether that person is someone who might become abusive. And that way you can stay out of abusive relationships and have a much better chance of dating someone who is respectful of you and your feelings. Jealousy and uncontrollable anger are never signs of love.

3

Who Are Date Abuse Victims and Why Does It Happen to Them?

My boyfriend would come into my classes at school and drag me out. He'd tell the teacher he was my probation officer. I was so embarrassed, but if I said anything, he'd beat me up.—Kathy, 14

He got real mad at me one night for dancing with this guy who was just a friend I'd known since kindergarten. So he pulled me by the hair to his car. Then he drove out in the woods, pushed me out of the car, and left me there.—Sheila, 15

The first time I knew something was wrong with Joyce was when she saw me hug my sister at school. My sister had won cheerleader. Joyce didn't know she was my sister because we'd only just started dating. She screamed at me and scratched my face so bad it bled. She said she'd get even with me if I left her.—Jonathan, 17

After we broke up, she wouldn't leave me alone. She'd phone and cry and say she was going to kill herself if I didn't start going with her again. I was scared out of my mind. I mean, what if she really killed herself? Maybe it would be my fault. So I'd say we could go back together just to get her not to do anything dumb.

Then a couple of weeks later I'd try to break up with her again. I'd say I didn't want to date only one girl. And I didn't think we had all that much in common. And she'd be happier dating someone else. The truth was, I just didn't want to date her. Don't I have a right to date who I want?

She kept up the suicide routine every time I broke up with her. I finally had to see a therapist to deal with how guilty I felt every time she threatened to kill herself.

Therapy helped a lot. I learned I wasn't responsible for her life.—Jason, 19

Why Do Victims of Date Abuse Stay in Violent Relationships?

The main reason is low self-esteem. These victims believe they are worthless and do not deserve to be treated better. Their self-esteem is so low that they desperately need someone—anyone—in order to feel good. These people may be fortunate enough to meet someone caring, respectful, and emotionally secure. But chances are just as likely that they will meet a date abuser. These victims are on a dating roulette wheel.

"I was dating for the first time," 15-year-old Susan said. "Jim was 18, a real hunk. I couldn't believe he was interested in me, the original Fat Kid On The Block. One night he said he was taking me bowling, but instead he parked on this hill out in the middle of nowhere. We started kissing. Then he pulled me down and forced me to have sex with him. I let him do it because I'd already let him kiss me and touch me above the waist. I thought he'd call me a tease if I told him to stop. And I didn't want him to break up with me, either. I thought it was pure luck that this guy wanted to date me, and I didn't believe for a minute anyone else ever would want to take me out."

When jealousy, possessiveness, and bullying are mistakenly believed to mean love, abuse is almost certain to follow. These date abuse victims believe that if their boyfriends or girlfriends want to constantly be with them, even to the exclusion of their other friends and activities, then their boyfriend or girlfriend must really love them. When the abuser expresses hurt that they are paying too much attention to other friends, or anger that they are flirting with another boy or girl, the victim feels it is good to be so wanted.

Some teenagers not only put up with abuse because they think they do not deserve better, but believe they themselves are quite worthless. To them, going out with anyone is better than not going out at all.

Low Self-Esteem

Low self-esteem is often the result of being raised by abusive parents. Whether these victims come from homes with alcoholic parents, battering parents, or parents who emotionally neglect them, they are left with the message that they are not good enough.

They believe that if *they* had been good enough they would not have been beaten, their parents would not have gotten drunk all the time, and they would have been loved. They have a deep sense of loss—of love, of nurturing, and of a normal family relationship.

These victims are so hungry for affection and love that they fall into dating relationships with anyone who will pay attention to them. Having never experienced parental love, they are unable to tell the difference between abuse and love. And if they were physically or sexually abused as children, the mixing of abuse with love reinforces their belief, however mistaken, that when someone loves you, you get hurt.

Abuse by Family Members

All types of abuse in one's family can lead to an acceptance or expectation of abuse in a dating relationship. Some victims were put down by family members because of their looks, being called fat, sloppy, lazy, stupid, or ugly. Some girls remember how their mothers were abused by their fathers, and they, in turn, expect the same from their boyfriends.

When people think little of themselves, others do the same. These victims often do not even realize they are in an abusive dating relationship. Therefore, they fall into abusive relationships over and over again. This does not mean they like to be abused, but rather that their values about relationships they learned in childhood lead them to find dating partners who will abuse them.

Some boys and girls from abusive families use dating as an escape from their home lives. They so desperately want someone to love them that they build up their boyfriends or girlfriends as the ideal solution to their problems at home. Then when their dates become abusive, they deny the abuse in order to keep up the imagined escape from abuse at home.

Pressure To be Like Everybody Else

Sometimes teenagers stay in abusive relationships because of pressure to be like everybody else. There is a push during adolescence to have a boyfriend or girlfriend. Many teenagers believe a major part of their status comes from having a steady relationship. There is also the intense romantic feeling that goes with dating someone regularly.

"It feels great to know you don't have to worry about who you're going out with Saturday night," Kimberly, 16, said. "My girlfriends who don't have a steady boyfriend spend all week waiting for the phone to ring. And if there's a party it's even worse 'cause they don't know if they're gonna go until they get a date."

Why Do These Victims Not Tell Someone About The Abuse?

Often, they fear that telling will cause their dates to hurt them more. Or, based on their poor self-image, they believe such treatment is justified. Or they feel guilty because their dates keep saying they can't live without them.

Many girls believe the old boy/girl rule that the girl is supposed to be responsible for keeping the relationship going. She is the one who is supposed to solve all the problems in the relationship. These girls confuse being a slave to their boyfriends with being in love. They believe they are supposed to do whatever the boy wants, including dressing and acting the way he wants. They even believe they deserve to be treated abusively if they do not do what their boyfriends want.

"He told me I deserved it, that I was such a slut and stuff. I started feeling like a slut," said Karen. "I missed school a lot, and my grades went down because I was always getting stomachaches. I never knew when he would hit me. Then I got depressed and all I wanted to do was stay in bed. It just seemed like everything kept going down, down, down."

Emotional abuse destroys victims' self-esteem so much that they agree to the demands of their dating partners because they feel they have no other options besides this relationship. Often the victim is told, "No one else will ever want you." The message is, "Even though you are worthless, because I love you I'll put up with you if you do what I say."

This type of humiliation and disrespect attacks the victim's feelings of self-worth. The attack is especially powerful coming from a person the victim loves and on whom he or she feels dependent.

The victims also feel ashamed, embarrassed, or afraid of what their parents will say if they tell them. Other times they think no one will believe them, or that others will say they were to blame. Still other victims have mistaken ideas about dating behaviors. They believe that if a date spends a lot of money on them, the date has a right to abuse them, even going so far as to demand sex with them.

Often victims of date abuse think if they stay in the relationship they will be able to get the person to become the kind of dating partner they want. This never happens. First, if the abuser is getting his or her way from the abusive behavior, why is there any need to change? Second, very few abusive people change without the help of a trained counselor. And third, people have to *want* to change their behavior. No one can *make* them change.

Alcohol or Drugs

Date abuse frequently occurs when one or both of the dating partners are under the influence of alcohol or drugs. Intoxicating or mind-altering substances change people's behavior. Someone who is drunk may show their anger with physical violence, a behavior they normally would not use while sober. Or, a boy who is high on drugs or alcohol may force sex on his date.

On the other hand, if you are dating an abusive person, you will be more vulnerable to taking the abuse if you yourself are high. When people are intoxicated their reflexes and thought processes do not work well. Therefore, if their date becomes abusive, they are not going to be alert enough to stop the abuse. And if a boy tries to force sex on his date, the girl may not have the strength to fight him off if she is high.

It is low self-esteem that keeps victims of date abuse seeking desperately to be loved. Too often, however, all they find is another abusive dating relationship. And the abuse only becomes stronger and more frequent as time passes.

Staying in an abusive relationship gets worse, never better. Dating becomes a prison—but a much more confining one than actual prison. Victims of date abuse are trapped behind invisible bars.

4

How to End an Abusive Dating Relationship and How to Prevent Future Date Abuse

My boyfriend told me if I ever broke up with him, he'd kill me. I dreaded going out with him because I knew he'd end up hitting me for something I didn't even know I did.—Sandra, 18

When I told Kim we couldn't date anymore because she was just too possessive and I needed space, she started following me around and telling other girls not to date me because I was crazy. I just couldn't get rid of her.—Steve, 17

Ending An Abusive Relationship

Ending an abusive dating relationship is not easy. The first step is to admit that you have been abused. The next step is to find out exactly *how* you have been abused. Then you will find it easier to end the abusive relationship and start healing the wounds of date abuse.

Being abused is being injured—and the wound has to heal before date abuse victims can trust that another boyfriend or girlfriend will not abuse them, too. This trust will come from being able to recognize a potentially abusive person and then deciding not to date that type of person.

To be aware that you are or have been a victim of date abuse, ask yourself the questions that follow. Answering yes to even one of them is a sign of date abuse. At the end of each type of abuse, ask yourself which incident hurt the most, and what happened? This will help you understand how you have been abused.

Physical Abuse

Has your boyfriend or girlfriend ever pushed, shoved, kicked, bitten, punched, beaten, or choked you? Has he or she ever thrown things at you, or threatened you with a weapon?

Sexual Abuse

Has your boyfriend or girlfriend ever bribed, tricked, or forced you to have sex? Did you have sex because you were afraid your date would become violent if you refused, or because you felt you owed sex to your date because of money spent on you?

Verbal Abuse

Has your date ever put you down, sworn at you, called you names, or threatened to harm you? Has he or she ever accused you of things you did not do, or exploded into a jealous, angry rage over a minor annoyance?

Emotional Abuse

Has your date ever given you the silent treatment or ignored you for long periods of time? Has your date frequently stood you up, broken dates, cheated on you, frightened you, or tricked you into believing they cared about you more than they actually did?

One idea to keep in mind as you think about ending an abusive relationship or making sure you do not get involved in another one is that *you cannot change another person's behavior.* People only change because they want to, not because you make them. That is why in order to heal the wounds of date abuse, to regain self-esteem, you need to know who *you* are. Are you shy, outgoing, lazy, energetic? What do you like and dislike about yourself? How would you go about changing what you don't like? What are your dreams? What are you good at? What are your weaknesses?

As you answer these questions, you will begin to appreciate your inner strengths, and to feel confident that you developed these strengths in order to take care of yourself.

Date abuse is a serious injury and like all injuries, there are wounds that have to heal before a person is completely well again.

Victim Blaming

Another thought to keep repeating to yourself is that *you are not to blame for the abuse.* No one deserves to be abused. For any reason. Self-blame, or victim-blaming, only lessens your self-worth and makes the abuser look good. When you feel guilty for imagined faults, you are giving the abuser permission to continue the abuse. And at the same time you are enabling the abuser to keep up his or her false self-image.

Remember, a date abuser will try to get you to accept the blame for abuse. They will say things like, "If you weren't so stupid, I wouldn't have to make all the plans," or, "If you didn't flirt with other guys all the time, I wouldn't get so mad and have to hit you."

To get rid of self-blame, try thinking positively about yourself in what are called affirmations. An affirmation is the belief that you do things for your own good, not to hurt others; that you do the best you can in any situation, but recognize that you will sometimes make mistakes.

Admitting to having made a mistake is not the same as blaming yourself. A self-blaming victim says things like, "If only I had paid more attention to her, she wouldn't have broken up with me," or, "It's all my fault he hit me because I was talking to this other boy."

Admitting a mistake, on the other hand, involves saying things like, "I was wrong when I thought he cared as much about me as I did about him," or, "Doing everything he wanted all the time was stupid." Remember, it is the *act* that was stupid, not *you*. When you can admit a mistake without blaming yourself for what your date did to you, you are off the victim-blaming route and on the road to self-esteem.

Victim-blaming often involves the unrealistic belief that we should have known what would happen in the future, even though there was no possible way we could have foreseen what happened. For example, suppose a boy asks a girl for a ride home from school. The boy is in several of her classes and seems nice. So she gives him a ride home. At his house, the girl goes inside to use the bathroom before driving home. The boy rapes her.

Is it the girl's fault that she was raped because she gave the boy a ride home? No. But she *did* make a mistake in giving the boy a ride. There was no way to know the boy would rape her. Her decision to give him a ride was based on her knowing him at school and her belief that he was a decent person. Without clues to tell her otherwise, how could she be blamed for giving him a ride? No way—unless she decides to blame herself rather than admitting she made a mistake.

Fear

Besides victim-blaming, there are other emotional wounds of date abuse that have to be healed. Fear is one. After being continually frightened by your date, it is normal to be afraid. This fear may take the form of recurring nightmares in which the abuser tries to hurt you. There is also a fear of dating someone else for fear the abuse will happen again. Many date abuse survivors believe the date abuse was a problem inside themselves, and thus assume the abuse *will* happen again. This assumption only intensifies the fear of dating other people.

Loss of Trust

A loss of trust in yourself is another result of date abuse that needs to be gotten rid of. People who believe they have poor judgment usually make poor judgments. What they fear will happen usually does. The more they do not trust themselves to date decent people, the more they date people who abuse them.

Jonathan, 15, dated a girl who constantly stood him up for no reason. One day she was "totally in love" with him. The next day she acted as if she did not know him. If he asked her out on those days, she either refused or stood him up. Jonathan finally quit asking her out.

But he was afraid the next girl he asked out would also stand him up. Because he did not trust his judgment to date a nonabusive girl, he ended up using poor judgment all the time and dated many abusive girls. By the time he was seventeen, this cycle had repeated itself so often that Jonathan did not believe he would ever be able to tell a decent girl from an abusive girl.

In the same way that a person who has been burned in a fire is afraid to go near a fire again, lack of trust in yourself can lead to lack of trust in others. Because dating relationships involve intimacy and trust, if that intimacy is violated, trust goes away. Some date abuse survivors end up hating all men or women. This type of mistrust is unhealthy. It makes the person constantly angry, and all their energy is filled with negative feelings. They cannot heal when there is so much negative baggage to carry around.

Destroyed Self-Esteem

Self-esteem is also destroyed as the result of an abusive dating relationship. Date abusers put down their partners and treat them as inferior, so it is understandable that people who get a daily dose of these put-downs end up not liking themselves. Everyone needs some outside feedback to confirm their feelings of self-worth. If our outside feedback is constantly negative, we doubt our worth, which leads to low self-esteem.

One boy said, "Before I dated her, I thought I could do anything. But she told me to shut me up every time I disagreed with her. That I didn't know what I was talking about, and I had the brains of an ape. The thought of losing her scared me so much I shut up and did things her way."

A girl said, "I put up with his abuse because I have a hard time believing I'm good enough *not* to put up with it."

When a person has high self-esteem, they can recognize when a boyfriend or girlfriend is trying to destroy their self-worth. Nancy, 16, said, "I know the difference between constructively criticizing someone and tearing her apart according to what you want her to be. I realized I had to get out of that relationship before I started believing his put-downs."

Depression and Addiction

Other wounds of date abuse are depression and addiction. Depression is caused by anger held inside. If you do not let out your anger, it turns into depression.

It is understandable how date abuse survivors become depressed if they have believed in the dating myth that falling in love means someone takes care of you and you live happily ever after.

No one lives happily ever after. All relationships take work. Relationships are like automobiles; if a car is not given regular tune-ups, it stops functioning properly. In relationships the tune-up is communication. If something your date does bothers you, say so. Keeping quiet only allows the abuse to continue. If your date cannot take hearing that something she or he does annoys you, then your date has a problem with not being in control. Always wanting to be in control comes from a feeling of insecurity. And insecurity and a need to be in control are problems that your dating partner must cope with; they are not your responsibility.

There is a big difference in *caring about* someone and *taking care of* them. Only infants and young children need taking care of. Mature teenagers take care of themselves. They care about the person they date, but they do not have to make sure their date is happy. Being happy is each individual's own responsibility.

When people are depressed for a long time, feelings of hopelessness and helplessness overcome them. If they are not able to get rid of their depression through some kind of therapy or counseling, they usually try to relieve the depression through using drugs, alcohol, food, smoking, or any other substance that gets rid of their painful feelings.

This type of substance abuse is called self-medicating. It does not cure the depression, and it is not a good idea. In date abuse cases, substance abuse is merely trading in one unhealthy addiction for another. After a breakup in a relationship, the addiction of needing to have a boyfriend or girlfriend around constantly is substituted with the addiction to a substance, such as alcohol or over eating. When date abuse victims recognize that addiction is a mask for depression, they can find healthy ways to feel good and be happy.

Healing the Wounds of Date Abuse

Although healing the wounds of date abuse begins with working on yourself, you do not have to go the whole way alone. Many date abuse survivors find help by talking to professional therapists—psychiatrists, psychologists, social workers, or other mental health counselors.

You can sound out such questions as, "How was I to know if I went into his house he'd rape me?" "What part of the rape was his responsibility?" "I got angry and said some mean things, but did that give him the right to hit me?" "It takes two people to make or break a relationship. I know my part. What was his part?" These professionals help date abuse victims put their experience in perspective, and learn ways to avoid falling into the date abuse trap again.

There are also group meetings for teenage date abuse survivors conducted by a trained counselor. It is helpful to learn that you are not the only one who has experienced date abuse, and that others have had many of the painful experiences you have.

Cindy, 19, said, "I've been in therapy with a psychologist for two years, and I don't get abused by boys anymore. Before therapy, I thought there was something really wrong with me if everyone I dated treated me bad. My psychologist helped me find lots of good stuff about myself, like what I'm good at and what I like and don't like in boys. That way I'll know before I start dating a guy whether he's decent."

Rachel, 16, said, "Before I started seeing my therapist, I never said anything negative to boys. But now I just speak right up and tell them they're doing something I don't like. And if they don't want to date me again, that's their problem. Because let me tell you, it may not be fun sitting home all the time, but it's sure better than getting a bloody nose or black eye all the time just to have a date."

Jeff, 17, said, "Before I joined this group of kids who'd been through date abuse, I didn't have anyone to talk to about what happened to me. My parents just thought my dating problems were 'part of adolescence' and would go away. The group is a great way to let it all hang out and have a bunch of other guys say, 'Yeah. That happened to me too, and what can we do about it?' "

Vicki, 15, said, "My therapist is really interested in me and whether or not I'm happy. I can tell her anything and she never puts me down. She doesn't tell me what to do, either. She lets me make my own decisions about dating. But we talk about everything first, and that helps me make my own decisions. It's like having a car that needs a new tire. If you don't have a jack, you can't fix it. So it's like she helps me find the tools to fix whatever's wrong."

Date Abuse Warning Signs

Be aware of date abuse warning signs. Does your date call several times a day to check up on you? Does he or she follow you around, keep you away from friends and family, or stop you from participating in outside activities?

Does he or she have a violent temper, becoming angry often, and for no reason? Out-of-control tempers can lead to physical abuse. No one has a right to hit you, no matter what you have done. If this happens, say immediately that if this ever happens again you two are finished. An abusive person won't want to continue seeing someone who is assertive and means what they say. So if phone calls for dates stop at this point, you will know that while he or she may have stopped calling, you have stopped an abusive dating situation from happening.

If you are in an abusive dating relationship and you want to get out of it, how do you break up with your boyfriend or girlfriend without the breakup resulting in even more abuse for you? It is understandable there would be an amount of fear and hesitation involved. For it is usually when someone breaks off the relationship that the abusive boyfriend or girlfriend becomes a major threat.

Things You Can Do

There are some things you can do to help make the breakup less potentially dangerous. First, make the break clean, definite, and final. Say, "I don't love you. Don't call me anymore," as opposed to a wishy-washy "I don't think we should date anymore." Never say, "You can call me sometime." The "sometime" gives a false message that you are open to dating that person again and allows the abuser to keep bothering you.

Most likely, the abuser will phone again to test your sincerity in breaking up. He or she may try to get you to agree to being just friends. The best response is not to speak to or see that person again, whether on the phone or in person. Arguing only encourages further abuse. So refuse to speak about your relationship, and cut off the abuse by hanging up or walking away from the abuser.

Second, if he or she begs you to meet just to talk, do not go. If you do, you will be putting yourself in a dangerous situation in which the abuser may hurt you. And this time the hurt will be more severe, because the abuser is already angry at you for breaking up. Third, do not allow your friends to carry notes back and forth between the two of you.

In extreme cases, you may want to change your phone number to an unlisted one, and have the locks on your doors changed in case the abuser has a key. Stay away from deserted places. And do not go places alone. Go out with a group instead. Experts do *not* advise carrying a weapon. It can be taken away and turned against you.

And most important: Take any threats very seriously. Keep a written record of any threats or actual harassment by the abuser. If there are witnesses, try to get statements from them. Any harassment at school should be reported to school officials. The police should also be told of any threats. Never rely on a court order to stop the abuser from harassing you. A restraining order is just a piece of paper, and the police usually hesitate to respond unless an act of violence has already occurred.

A Healthy Relationship

So, what is a healthy dating relationship? In a healthy relationship, both people want the other to grow and develop to their fullest potential. Each partner encourages the other's pleasure in close friendships with other people, and feels joy in the other's accomplishments and independent activities.

There is no possessive desire to be with each other every minute of the day. While they love each other, neither partner feels they *need* the other in order to live. Each partner feels self-worth, and neither tries to control the other.

There are five essentials for a healthy relationship:
- Respect
- Trust
- Support
- Fair fights
- Feeling relaxed with each other

Respect

Respect means that you each care about the other person and you also care about yourself. You respect each other's decisions. Where there is mutual respect, there are no put-downs or sarcastic remarks.

Trust

Trust in a healthy relationship means there are no lies, manipulations, or secrets. There is room for each to have other friends without the fear that these other friendships will lessen your own relationship. Trust also means that you can share your feelings without fearing that the other person may blackmail you with something you revealed. In a healthy relationship, you want to share your feelings and past experiences because you trust your date to be as careful with your feelings as she or he is with their own.

Support

Support in a healthy relationship means that each person listens to what the other says. Each recognizes that no one is perfect, and minor annoyances are accepted. You are there for each other during both good and bad times.

Fair Fighting

Fair fighting means that when arguments happen, as they do in every relationship, certain rules allow each person to come out of the argument feeling all right:

No physical aggression is allowed. The argument centers on what the problem is *now*, not what happened last month. (The old stuff should already have been worked out, and now, in the heat of emotions, is not the time to rehash it.) No name-calling is allowed. Name-calling is merely an attempt to steer the argument away from the real issue.

Stay on the topic and talk about what you are feeling. Use "I statements" to say what you are angry about and what you need. Say, "I don't like it when you . . ." or, "I need such-and-such from you," instead of, "You're always doing. . .," or, "You should do such-and-such."

Relaxation

Relaxation in a healthy relationship means that both people feel relaxed because they do not worry that the other person may suddenly abuse them. You can laugh at yourselves without putting each other down. You are not afraid to say what is on your mind.

In a healthy relationship, arguments are not won or lost; rather, arguments are settled. And all problems can be worked out because behind any problem are two people who truly care about each other.

5

Date Rape: What to Do If It Happens to You

I never expected Jeff to hurt me. He'd always been nice to me. Our first two dates were so romantic—a canoeing picnic on the lake and horseback riding in the mountains. He'd never tried anything past kissing.

Then, on our third date, he took me to a beach party. I thought there would be lots of couples there. But there was only one other couple, friends of Jeff's I didn't know. Jeff took me to a private spot down the beach where we could watch the waves and look at the stars.

He started kissing me. It was great at first, but then he started pulling my shirt up and trying to touch me. I told him to stop, I didn't want to do this. But he just kept on, saying all girls said no but meant yes. I tried to push him away, but he pulled my shorts off and got on top of me. I screamed, but nobody was around to hear. I tried to scratch him and kick him, but he was bigger than me, and he held me down. It seemed like hours.

Afterwards, he acted like nothing had happened. He wanted to know if I wanted to go out next week. Can you believe that? He'd just raped me, and now he wanted to know if I wanted to go out with him again.

At home, I got in the shower for over an hour. But I still didn't feel clean. I was afraid to tell my parents. What if they thought it was my fault? I felt dirty and bad. How could I have been so stupid as not to know what Jeff was really like?—Karen, 15

It is estimated that one in five girls in the United States will be raped on a date—which means one rape takes place every thirty seconds. However, only about 5 percent of victims report the crime.

What is Rape?

Any forced sexual activity is rape, from kissing to intercourse. And rape is a crime. In addition, both women *and* men may be raped. Many people wrongly believe that only homosexual men are raped, and that rapes against men are committed only by homosexual men. These are myths, not facts.

Many rape victims say, "I'm strong. This is no big deal. I can handle it. I'll just forget it ever happened." But these victims do not forget.

If you have been raped, the first thing you need to know and believe is that *it was not your fault*—whether you were assaulted by a stranger or by someone you know. Rape is not your fault, even if you were under the influence of drugs or alcohol at the time, or doing something risky, like hitchhiking. *Rape is never the fault of the victim. No person asks to be raped or deserves to be raped.*

What Should You Do If You Are the Victim of Date Rape?

Do not bathe, shower, or douche. Save the clothes you were wearing. Semen, skin, hairs, and clothing fibers can be collected and used as evidence against your attacker. With DNA testing, any semen, saliva, hair, or skin can be compared to those of the attacker. A match is proof of the attacker's identity. It is vital that this evidence be collected as soon as possible, as the DNA in semen can only be identified for up to 48 hours.

Go to a rape crisis center or hospital emergency room. A rape crisis center provides 24-hour free support, counseling, information, and referrals for rape survivors. Trained counselors help you deal with your feelings, make decisions about medical and legal matters, and obtain needed follow-up care. The counselors may go with you to the hospital, the police, or court.

Rape crisis centers and hot lines are listed at the end of this book. Emergency phone numbers can also be found in the front of the telephone directories, or by calling information, or by dialing 911.

Even if you do not want to report the attack to the police, getting medical care is important in order to determine if you have been injured. Rape victims may be in shock and may not be aware of injuries. Medical tests can determine if you have contracted a venereal disease or the AIDS virus, or if you are pregnant.

What Happens at the Hospital Emergency Room?

First, you will see an admitting clerk. The clerk will take your name, address, age, and the reason you are there. You do not need to give all the details of the assault. But you do have to say you were sexually assaulted in order to receive proper treatment.

You will be asked to sign consent forms for taking medical evidence. This might include taking photos of torn clothing or of your injuries. You will be asked to undress so that your clothes can be saved for evidence. You may be asked to sit on a piece of paper and comb your pubic hair. The loose hairs that fall onto the paper may contain semen that can be used for DNA testing.

You will be asked what sexual acts were forced on you. It is quite normal to feel uncomfortable or embarrassed by this. You may want to point to pictures rather than talk in detail about what happened. Feel free to ask any question you want.

Your medical history, date of last menstrual period, blood pressure, pulse, and temperature will be taken. The doctor will listen to your heart, examine your breasts, and check for injuries, such as bruises, cuts, blood, and traces of semen on the outside of your vaginal area.

Next, you will be given a pelvic examination. This is the same procedure that you have had from your regular doctor. The exam may feel uncomfortable as the doctor examines the vagina, the same area where you have been assaulted. It is helpful to take deep breaths in and out and, if possible, try to think about some other, happy, time in your life that has nothing to do with rape.

If you are reporting the crime, the medical evidence will be given to the police. It is a good idea to let the doctor take the evidence even if you are not reporting the rape. The evidence can be stored at the hospital and be available if you decide to prosecute later. Collecting evidence is a painless procedure. The doctor wipes cotton swabs over the inside of the mouth, vagina, and rectum.

Blood will be drawn to test for venereal disease or the AIDS virus. Be sure to check back with the emergency room for results. If you have a venereal disease, you will need treatment. You may also be asked for a urine sample to test for pregnancy. You should be offered options for the prevention of pregnancy. If you are not, be sure to ask.

You should have two follow-up treatments, two weeks and four weeks after your emergency-room exam. These treatments are necessary to recheck for pregnancy, venereal disease, or AIDS.

During the medical procedure, you have certain rights: You have the right to be examined without your parents being notified, and without any law enforcement officers being in the examining room; to request that a friend, relative, or rape crisis counselor be with you; to phone your personal physician; to request that a female physician examine you; and to refuse the collection of medical evidence.

You have the right to ask that each medical procedure be explained to you before it is done. And you may request copies of all medical reports.

Most important of all, you have the right to strict medical confidentiality. This means that details of the rape are between you and the doctor who examines you. The doctor may not tell your parents or anyone else without your permission.

What About Telling the Police?

The emergency room usually contacts the police automatically. But you still have the right *not* to make a crime report. However, the more victims who report being raped, the more rapists will be caught, and the better the chances of stopping this violent crime. Bear in mind, too, that if you do not report the rape, your attacker will be free to hurt others. But most importantly, if you do not talk about what happened, you may never fully recover.

Although it will be emotionally difficult for you to recall and describe exactly what happened, you should be prepared to be asked by the police to repeat the details of being raped many times.

The first step in reporting rape is to fill out a crime report. In a few days, police officers may call you into their office or visit you at your home for a follow-up report. If you are not sure of something, say so. Ask any questions you want. The police will need to know what sexual acts were forced upon you in order to know what crimes can be charged. Although you feel embarrassed, remember that *you* are not the person who did these things. Your attacker did.

You have certain rights in dealing with the police as well. You have the right to ask to be interviewed by a female officer; to read everything the police write on forms and to ask them to correct any errors; to have restraining orders issued against your attacker; and to be given reasonable protection, such as an escort to and from court, or an additional police patrol assigned to your neighborhood.

Be sure to get the names and badge numbers of the police officers who interview you. If you remember anything else about the incident later on, you can phone them.

What about your legal rights? You have the right to report the crime, but not to prosecute. However, if the district attorney prosecutes the case, you may be called as a witness. You have the right to withdraw your testimony against your attacker at any time. You also have the right to sue a company for negligence if you were sexually assaulted in a place that has unsafe conditions, such as an underlighted parking lot.

If you choose to press charges, and the case is prosecuted, you have the right to request that your attorney be present during the proceedings; to be asked only those questions that are relevant to your rape; to request that the prosecutor not permit questions about your prior sexual experience with anyone other than your attacker; to have copies of any court records; and, if your attacker is sent to jail, to request to be informed of his parole and/or release dates.

You have the right to sue the suspect in civil proceedings. If you are a minor, you have the right to testify in the judge's chambers, and to have your parents excused from the courtroom during your testimony.

What Happens in Court?

Usually the events follow this pattern:

You file a crime report with the police. If you do not know your attacker personally, you may look at mugshots or help a police artist make a composite picture. When the suspect is arrested, you may be required to identify him in a lineup.

The police present the case to the prosecutor, who may ask you questions. The prosecutor decides whether there is enough evidence to issue a formal complaint. If there is, the suspect is arraigned (called to appear) before a judge. If the suspect pleads not guilty, a hearing is set, usually ten days after the arraignment. You may be asked to testify.

During the hearing, only the basic details of the rape are discussed. What must be established is that the rape occurred, and that there is reason to believe this suspect did it without your consent. If the judge at the arraignment decides there is enough evidence, the case goes to trial.

If the suspect pleads guilty, he is charged and sentenced without a trial. If not, a pretrial hearing is held to pick the jury. Due to delays called by the defense attorney, it may be months or even a year or longer before the trial actually starts.

When the trial begins, you will testify as a witness. Be sure to phone the prosecutor's office the day before your appearance to learn of any delays in the proceedings so you will not make an unnecessary trip to court.

In addition to the prosecuting attorney, the defense attorney will question you. He or she will try to discredit you in order to defend the suspect. The defense attorney may suggest that you are mistaken in your identification of the suspect, or that you are lying and had sex willingly with the suspect. Do not be intimidated by the questions. Just tell the truth. The defense attorney is simply doing the best job to defend the suspect.

In court, it is not *you versus the rapist:* your role there is as a witness. The "people of the state" prosecute the suspect, because the suspect is charged with committing a crime under the laws of the state. The attorney prosecuting the case is a deputy from the prosecutor's office.

After all testimony has been given, the jury finds the suspect either guilty or innocent. If he is found guilty, a hearing is set for the sentencing.

In addition to criminal proceedings, you may also sue your attacker for damages in a civil suit. Unlike a criminal suit, which requires that a jury find the defendant guilty "beyond a reasonable doubt," a civil suit only requires "a preponderance of evidence." In a civil suit, you will have to hire and pay for your own attorney.

What Are Your Financial Rights?

Most states have a Victims' Assistance Program (V.A.P.), through which you may apply for financial aid in meeting your medical or legal expenses. Check with the district attorney's office, the public prosecutor's office, or a local rape crisis center to find out if your state has a V.A.P., and if so how to apply. Remember, however, you usually have to report the crime to the police in order to qualify. And you must file a claim within one year of the assault to receive financial benefits.

In California, for example, you may get up to $10,000 for medical and hospital expenses that are not paid by your health insurance. Medical expenses may include the cost of therapy with a psychological counselor. You may also receive up to $500 for attorney fees. Some states' Victim Assistance Programs will also pay medical expenses for any immediate family member who was present at the crime and needs medical or psychological care as a result.

Professional Counseling

Today, after professional counseling and attending a rape survivors' workshop, Karen, the fifteen-year-old who was raped on her third date with Jeff, says, "If a boy tried to rape me today, I would know that no guy is allowed to touch me without my consent. If I could give advice to other girls I'd say the most important thing is when that little voice inside says, 'I'm scared,' listen to that voice. Chances are that voice is right.

"Speak up for yourself. Don't be afraid to say, 'No. Don't touch me.' After I was raped, I felt so ashamed, as if I deserved to be raped. But I didn't. You don't. No one does."

Afteraffects of Date Rape

Victims of date rape experience many of Karen's emotions—shame, guilt, fear, self-doubt. They doubt their ability to judge people's characters. They find it difficult to trust others. And, naturally, they face the frightening prospect of seeing their attacker again because they might know him or her.

Victims worry about telling what happened for fear they will be blamed or that their friends will stop being their friends. They worry about reporting the crime to the police, and about prosecuting their assailant for fear the rapist will get even with them.

Rape is a violent act in which the victim is powerless. It is quite natural to have conflicting, violent emotions following such an attack. You may feel as if you have lost control of your life.

These symptoms are normal, and are part of what is called RTS, or Rape Trauma Syndrome. RTS is similar to Post-Traumatic Stress Syndrome (PTSD), which many soldiers feel after returning from battles in which they have killed the enemy and lived in constant fear that they will be killed. RTS can occur days, months, or years after the rape.

Other RTS symptoms include flashbacks, in which the victims re-experience the rape while fully awake; anxiety attacks in which they feel as if they are suffocating; difficulty in concentrating; problems with memory; or nightmares in which the victims relive the rape.

You may either lose your appetite or overeat, sleep all the time or not be able to sleep, be afraid of being alone or be afraid of being in crowds. In addition, you may experience physical symptoms such as nausea, stomachaches, headaches, or pain in muscles or joints.

Many teenage survivors of date rape experience severe depression. They withdraw from friends and from activities that used to give them pleasure. They feel guilty because they knew their attacker, and were not able to foresee or stop the rape. Or they feel so angry at what happened that they want to hurt the attacker. They want to escape, to forget, to have their life the way it was before the rape.

Other rape survivors stop studying, cut classes, or start self-destructive behavior, such as taking drugs or alcohol, or performing risky activities such as driving too fast.

One date rape survivor said, "I see people and wonder what they think. Maybe they wonder whether I was careful enough, whether I caused it in any way, whether I fought hard enough. I wonder the same things."

Another said, "I don't want to think about anything. Except being safe. Will he come back? I feel helpless to stop him if he does. Sometimes I feel like I'm going crazy."

And yet another girl said, "I wonder if I'll ever be able to date a boy again. Right now the idea of kissing a guy or having him touch me makes me sick."

Like this survivor, most date rape victims are afraid their attacker will return and hurt them again. In reality, although rapists may threaten to return, few rapists ever do. Yet taking time to make your home safe is one way of dealing with such fears.

Some Safety Precautions

For example, change all locks in your house. Put deadbolts on all doors and windows. Install a peephole in your front door to see who is there *before* opening the door. And never open the door to a stranger, such as someone who says he is a repairman. Ask the person to hold an I.D. up to a window. Then check that I.D. by phoning the person's workplace to make sure he or she does indeed work there and is really supposed to be at your house. If the stranger argues, call the police.

If a stranger asks to use your phone because of car trouble or some other emergency, make the call yourself while the stranger waits outside. Again, if the stranger argues, call the police. Put emergency phone numbers next to all your phones.

There are some safety precautions to use outdoors as well. Research shows that people who stand straight, walk with a firm step, look ahead rather than down, and act as if they know where they are going are less likely to be seen as possible assault victims. Attackers look for people who appear weak and unsure of themselves. If a stranger, or even someone you know, stops to ask a question, it is okay to say you don't know or not to answer at all.

While walking outside, make sure you can move easily while carrying packages. Some women use packages as weapons to throw at attackers. If you think you are being followed, turn around and check. Then cross the street, yell, and run to the nearest lighted and crowded area.

These actions may force the attacker to stop following you.

Think about places where you might be vulnerable to assault: elevators, laundry rooms, parking lots. Never go into any of these places at night alone. Look at who is already in the elevator when you are about to get on. If someone looks suspicious, wait for the next elevator.

If someone attacks you, yell as loud as you can and make a scene. Some experts recommend yelling, "Fire!" because people respond fast to a fire, whereas if you are with a date and yell, "Help!", people might merely think you are teasing each other or having a "lovers' quarrel." Other experts think yelling "Fire!" might cause a dangerous stampede in a crowded place. So they recommend yelling, "Rape!"

Before getting into your car, first check the front and back seats. If anyone is inside, run away. Then phone the police. If your car breaks down, open the hood and tie a white cloth to the antenna. Then stay in your locked car with the windows rolled up.

When someone stops to help you, stay in your locked car and ask them to call the police. If you feel threatened, say someone else stopped earlier and has already called the police, who are on their way.

If you think you are being followed while driving your car, do not drive home. You do not want strangers knowing where you live or attacking you as you get out of the car. Instead, drive to the nearest police station or public place. Then keep honking the horn and yelling.

If you ride the bus, stay awake. Notice who gets on and off. And always carry money for emergency phone calls.

As to weapons, remember that any weapon can be taken from you in an attack and used against you. Or you may not have your weapon with you when you need it. Approximately half of all date rape attacks occur in the home. Tear gas or Mace may not work when you need them. As an alternative to weapons, enroll in a self-defense course. Self-defense can turn fear into anger and anger into action.

Awareness and Assertiveness

Remember, the key words in self-protection are *awareness* of your surroundings and *assertiveness* of your needs and rights.

Some girls give in to rape because the boy makes them feel they should, by saying things like, "If you loved me, you'd have sex with me." Or, "Everybody does it." Or, "How could you let me get all excited and not go all the way? I can't stop myself now."

Some girls believe if the boy is aroused and the girl stops the petting at that point, the boy will be physically damaged because he was not able to ejaculate. This is not true. The boy may feel discomfort for a short time, but no permanent physical damage will occur. The discomfort comes from the fact that when aroused, the tissues of the sex organs fill with blood. This causes both the penis and the vagina to swell.

During orgasm, the blood is released back into the body and the swelling goes down. When a man or woman is aroused, but their arousal does not lead to orgasm, it just means the man or woman has to wait for the excitement to die down and the blood to go back into the body by itself. Not reaching orgasm after being sexually aroused does not cause permanent injuries.

No Means No

No means no. However, in fairness, a word must be said about "Saying No." Remember that when someone is in the middle of sex, certain body chemicals take over. The boy loses control of his actions. This loss of control is a natural part of sex. Therefore, if a girl changes her mind about having sex in the middle of intercourse, she cannot count on the boy's even being able to hear her say no.

Being an adult means being responsible for your actions. If you do not want to have sex, say no before the lovemaking reaches "the point of no return."

Date rape victims have found help in talking to a psychologist, psychiatrist, social worker, or other rape crisis counselor. These people are trained to listen without judging. They can help you deal with your feelings in the way that is best for you. Remember, not talking about rape will not make it go away.

Ways To Help Prevent Date Rape

There are ways to help prevent date rape. First, whenever you have a date, make sure you tell someone who you are going out with and where you are going. If a boy invites you to his house, make sure someone else will be there too—a parent, sibling, or friend.

If you start to feel uncomfortable on a date *for any reason,* trust your instincts. Do whatever you have to do to get out of the situation safely. If a boy starts coming on too strong, or if he tries to force himself on you sexually, speak with a firm, strong voice. Make it *very* clear that you want him to stop. If you speak in a giggly, soft voice, you are giving him mixed signals. He may think you are playing hard to get that you are indeed saying no, but meaning yes.

Always stay in control of your senses. If you use drugs or alcohol, your judgment will become clouded, and you will have a harder time getting out of an unsafe situation. Learn how to defend yourself by enrolling in a self-defense class or rape-prevention workshop. You have the right to ask for whatever you need to make the transition from date rape victim to date rape survivor.

If you expect no less than equality and decency when it comes to treatment by teachers, friends, and bosses, it makes sense to expect no less than equality and decency in your dating relationships. You belong only to you. Nobody has a right to violate your body or mind in any way. Getting a boy's or girl's love is never worth that big a price.

When you fall in love, *you* matter, the person you fall in love with matters, and *what you do with the rest of your life* matters most of all.

Bibiliography

Books:

Bouchard, Elizabeth. *Sexual Harassment.* New York: Rosen Publishing, 1990.

Fay, Jennifer F. *Top Secret: Sexual Assault Information for Teenagers.* Kent, WA: King County Sexual Assault Resource Center, 1988.

Levy, Barrie. *Dating Violence: Young Women in Danger.* Seattle, WA: Seal Press, 1991.

McShane, Claudette. *Warning! Dating May Be Hazardous to Your Health.* Racine, WI: Mother Courage Press, 1988.

Periodicals:

Dobie, Kathy, "Between Seduction and Rape." *Vogue,* Dec. 1991, 154–160.

Elkind, David. "Acquaintance Rape." *Parents,* April 1989, 197–199.

Kessner, Ellen Zelda. "Sweeetheart Murders." *Redbook,* March, 1988, 130–188.

Kirsch, Robin J. *Educational Print and Outreach Pamphlet,* WGBH, 1992.

Leo, John. "When the Date Turns Into Rape." *Time.* Mar. 23, 1987, 77.

Appendix A

Your Dating Rights

You have the right to:

- Say no
- Trust yourself above all others
- Receive decent treatment by your date
- Be safe on a date
- Disagree with your date
- Be assertive with your date
- Have mutually consenting and pleasurable sex
- Refuse to have sex
- Get angry
- Leave a date when your instincts tell you to
- Prosecute for battery and sexual assault
- Have a healthy dating relationship
- Be loved

Appendix B

Hotlines and Crisis Centers

To find the rape crisis service closest to you, use this guide or contact your local information operator, women's center, or law enforcement agency. A general list of hotlines are listed first, followed by a state by state listing for the United States. Listings for Canadian provinces follow the United States list. If there is no rape crisis service in your immediate area, you can contact the nearest hotline. Some rape crisis centers will accept collect calls. Following the Canadian listings you will find a guide to Victim Assistance Programs in the United State.

This list is a partial listing from the National Directory of Rape Prevention and Treatment Resources. To obtain a complete list, write to: NCPCR, U.S. Department of Health and Human Services, National Institute of Mental Health, 5600 Fishers Lane, Rockville, MD 20857 (301) 443-1910.

An asterisk (*) after a phone number indicates that it is a hotline. All hotlines are 24-hour.

Youth Crisis Hot Line
(800) 448-4663

Teen Hotline

(800) 855-4673

Child Help, USA
(800) 422-4453

UNITED STATES

Alabama

Rape Response Program
3600 8th Ave. South
Birmingham, AL 35222
(205) 323-7273*

**Council Against Rape/
Lighthouse**
830 S. Court St,
P.O. Box 4622
Montgomery, AL 36104
(205) 263-4481
9:00 AM–7:00 PM
24-hour services (through
referral network)

Alaska

**Standing Together
Against Rape**

111 E. 13th St.
Anchorage, AK 99510
(907) 276-7273 *(hotline)*
(907) 277-0222 *(week nights,
weekends)*

**Women in Crisis—
Counseling and
Assistance, Inc. (WICCA)**
331 Fifth Ave.
Fairbanks, AK 99701
(907) 452-7273 (hotline)
(907) 452-2293 *(office)*

**Bering Sea Women's
Group**
P.O. Box 1596
Nome, AK 99762
(907) 443-5444*

Arizona

Center Against Sexual Assault (CASA)
5555 N. 7th
Phoenix, AZ 85013
(602) 257-8095 (hotline)
(602) 279-9824 (office)
8:30 AM–7:00 PM

Crisis Intervention Unit
Scottsdale Police Department
3739 Civic Center
Scottsdale, AZ 85251
(602) 994-2593

Tucson Rape Crisis Center, Inc.
P.O. Box 843
Tucson, AZ 85702
(602) 623-7273 (hotline)
(602) 624-7273 (office)

Arkansas

Rape Crisis, Inc.
P.O. Box 5181,
Hillcrest Station
Little Rock, AR 72205
(501) 375-5181*

Bay Area Women Against Rape
1515 Webster
Oakland, CA 94612
(415) 845-7273 (hotline)
(415) 465-3890 (office)

Rape Counseling Service of Fresno, Inc.
3006 N. Fresno St.
Fresno, CA 93703
(209) 222-7273 (hotline)
(209) 227-1880 (office)
8:30 AM–5:00 PM

Los Angeles Commission on Assaults Against Women
Los Angeles Rape and Battering Hotline
c/o Women's Center at
Council House
543 N. Fairfax Ave.
Los Angeles, CA 90036
(213) 392-8381 (hotline)
(213) 938-3661 (office)
9:00 AM–5:00 PM

Rape Crisis Center of the Monterey Peninsula
P.O. Box 862
Monterey, CA 93940
(408) 375-4357*

Sacremento Rape Crisis Center
2224 J. St.
Sacramento, CA 95816
(916) 447-7273 *(hotline)*
(916) 447-3223 *(office)*

San Bernardino Rape Crisis Intervention Services
1875 N. "D" St.
San Bernardino, CA 92405
(714)882-5291 (hotline)
(714) 883-8689 *(office)*
9:00 AM–5:00 PM

San Francisco Women Against Rape
3543 18th St.
San Francsico, CA 941110
(415) 647-7273*
3:00 PM–7:00 AM *(counseling)*

Child and Adolescent Sexual Abuse Resource Center
San Francisco General Hospital
Bldg 80, Ward 83, Rm. 318
1001 Potrero
San Francisco, CA 94110
(415) 821-8386
9:00 AM–5:00 PM *(counseling)*
24-hour medical services

Marin Rape Crisis Center
P.O. Box 392
San Rafael, CA 94902
(415) 924-2100*

Santa Cruz Women Aainst Rape
P.O. Box 711
Santa Cruz, CA 95061
(408) 426-7273*

Rape Treatment Center
Santa Monica Hospital
Medical Center
1225 15th St.
Santa Monica, CA 90404
(213) 451-1511
24-hour services

Rape Crisis Center of Sonoma County
P.O. Box 1426
Santa Rosa, CA 95402
(707) 545-7273 (hotline)
(707) 545-7270 (office)
9:00 AM–5:00 PM

Rape Crisis Center of San Joaquin County
930 N. Commerce
Stockton, CA 95202
(209) 465-4997 *(hotline)*
(209) 941-2611 *(office)*

Colorado

Sexual Assault Task Force
Aspen Mental Health Clinic
P.O. 2330
Aspen, CO 81611
(303) 925-5400*

Health and Hospitals Mental Health Program
Social Services Department
W. 8th Ave. and Cherokee
Denver, CO 80204
(303) 893-7001
24-hour services

Connecticut

**Hartford YWCA Sexual
Assault Crisis Service**
135 Broad St.
Hartford, CT 06105
(203) 525-1163 or
522-6666*

Delaware

**Rape Crisis Center of
Wilmington**
P.O. Box 1507
Wilmington, DE 19899
(302) 658-5011*

District of Columbia (Washington, D.C.)

Sexual Offense Branch
Metropolitan Police Department
300 Indiana Ave., N.W.
Washington, DC 20001
(202) 727-4151
24-hour services

Florida

Hubbard House
222 E. Duval
Jacksonville, FL 32202
(904) 354-3114*

Rape Treatement Center
1611 N.W. 12th Ave.
Miami, FL 33136
(305) 325-6949*

Georgia

Rape Crisis Center
Grady Memorial Hospital
80 Butler St., S.E.
Atlanta, GA 30335
(404) 588-4861*

Rape Crisis Center of the Coastal Empire, Inc.
P.O. Box 8492
Savannah, GA 31412
(912) 233-7273*

Idaho

Rape Crisis Alliance
720 W. Washington St.
Boise, ID 83702
(208) 345-7273*

Illinois

Code R Program

Billings Hospital of the
University of Chicago
Hospitals and Clinics
Box 215, 950 E. 59th St.
Chicago, IL 60637
(312) 962-6246
24-hour services

Women in Crisis Can Act, Inc. (WICCA)

1628A W. Belmont
Chicago, IL 60657
(312) 929-5150 *(hotline)*
(312) 528-3303 *(office)*
5:00–11:00 PM Tues-Fri

Crisis Intervention and Referral Service

Evanston Hospital
2650 Ridge Ave.
Evanston, IL, 60201
(312) 492-6500*

Rape Information and Counseling Service (RICS)

P.O. Box 2211
Springfield, IL 62705
(217) 753-8081 *(hotline)*
(217) 753-0133 *(office)*

Indiana

Calumet Women United Against Rape

P.O. Box 2617
Gary, IN 46403
(219) 937-0450, 980-4207, and
769-3141 *(local hotline)*
24-hour hotlines

Crisis Intervention Service

Gallahue Mental Health Center
Community Hospital of
Indianapolis, Inc.
1500 N. Ritter Ave.
Indianapolis, IN 46219
(317) 353-5947 *(hotline)*
(317) 353-5457 *(emergency room)*
(317) 353-5931 *(office)*
8:30 AM–5:00 PM

Lifeline
200 S. Sixth St.
Terre Haute, IN 47807
(812) 235-8333 *(hotline)*
(812) 238-2620 *(office)*

Iowa

**Story County Sexual
Assault Care Center**
P.O. Box 1150, ISU Station
Ames, IA 50010
(515) 292-1101*

**Rape Crisis Services—
YWCA**
318 5th St., S.E.
Cedar Rapids, IA 52401
(319) 363-5490 *(hotline)*
(319) 365-1458 *(YMCA)*

Kansas

**Douglas County Rape Victim
Support Service, Inc.**
1035 Pennsylvania
Lawrence, KS 66044
(913) 841-2345 *(hotline)*
(913) 843-8985 *(office)*
1:00 PM–4:00 PM

**Wichita Area Rape Center,
Inc.**
1801 E. 10th St.
Wichita, KS 67214
(316) 263-3002 *(hotline)*
(316) 268-0185 *(office)*
8:30 AM–5:00 PM

Kentucky

Lexington Rape Crisis Center
P.O. Box 1603
Lexington, KY 40592
(606)253-2511 *(hotline)*
(606) 252-8514 *(office)*
8:00 AM–5:00 PM

R.A.P.E. Relief Center
604 S. 3rd St.
Louisville, KY 40202
(502) 581-7273*
24-hour hotline

Louisiana

Work Against Rape—Sexual Assault Care Service/ HELPLINE
1407 Murray St., #204
Alexandria, LA 71301
(318) 445-4357 *(hotline)*
(318) 445-2022 *(office)*
8:00 AM–5:00 PM

YWCA Rape Crisis Service
601 S. Jefferson Davis Pkwy.
New Orleans, LA 70119
(504) 483-8888 *(hotline)*
(504) 488-2693 *(office)*
9:00 AM–5:00 PM

Stop Rape Crisis Center
East Baton Rouge Parish
District Attorney's Office
215 St. Louis St., #307
Baton Rouge, LA 708801
(504) 389-3456*

Maine

**The Rape Crisis Center
of Greater Portland**
193 Middle St.
Portland, ME 04101
(207) 774-3613 *(hotline)*
(207) 774-4305 *(office)*

Maryland

**Baltimore Center for Victims
of Sexual Assault**
128 W. Franklin St.
Baltimore, MD 21201
(301) 366-7273 *(hotline)*
(301) 685-0937 *(office)*

**Community Crisis Center
Sexual Assault Services**
4910 Auburn Ave.
Bethesda, MD 20814
(301) 656-9449 *(hotline)*
(301) 656-9526 *(office)*

Massachusetts

**Counselors/Advocates
Against Rape**
Everywoman's Center
Wilder Hall, University of
Massachusetts
Amherst, MA 01003
(413) 545-0800 *(hotline)*
(413) 545-0883 *(office)*

**Rape Crisis Intervention
Program**
Beth Israel Hospital
330 Brookline Ave.
Boston, MA 02215
(617) 735-3337 *(emergency)*
(617) 7335-4645 *(information)*
9:00 AM–5:00 PM
24-hour services

Michigan

Assault Crisis Center
4009 Washtenaw Rd.
Ann Arbor, MI 48104
(313) 994-1616 (hotline)
(313) 971-9780 (office)
8:30 AM–5:00 PM

Rape Counseling Center
Detroit Police Department
4201 St. Antoine, Rm. 838
Detroit, MI 48201
(313) 224-4487 (hotline)
(313) 832-2530 (office)

Domestic Violence and Sexual Assault Crisis Center
YWCA
310 E. 3rd St.
Flint, MI 48502
(313) 238-7233*
9:00 AM–5:00 PM

Rape Crisis Center
1330 Bradford
Grand Rapids, MI 49503
(616) 774-3535*

Minnesota

Aid to Victims of Sexual Assault
2 E. 5th St.
Duluth, MN 55805
(218) 727-8538 *(hotline—Duluth)*
(800) 232-1300 *(toll-free)*
(218) 727-4353 *(office)*
8:00 AM–4:30 PM

Rape and Sexual Assault Center
1222 W. 31st St.
Minneapolis, MN 55408
(612) 825-4357*
9:00 AM–7:30 PM

Women's Advocates
584 Grand
St. Paul, MN 55102
(612) 227-8284
24-hour services

Mississippi

Gulf Coast Women's Center
P.O. Box 333
Biloxi, MS 39533
(601) 435-1968

Department of Mental Health
Division of Community Services
1101 Robert E. Lee Bldg.
Jackson, MS 39201
(601) 359-1301

Missouri

Sexual Assault Treatment Center
St. Lukes Hospital
Emergency Room
4400 Wornall Rd.
Kansas City, MO 64111
(816) 932-2171
24-hour service

Rape Crisis Assistance, Inc.
P.O. Box 1611
Springfield, MO 65805
(417) 866-1969*

Sex Crime Section
St. Louis Police Department
1200 Clark Ave.
St. Louis, MO 63103
(314) 444-5385
24-hour services

Montana

Bilings Rape Task Force
1245 N. 29th St., Rm. 218
Billings, MT 59101
(406) 259-6506*

Woman's Support Line
Rape Awareness Program
Helena Woman's Center
146 E. 6th Ave.
Helena, MT 59601
(406) 443-5353*

Women's Place
127 E. Main, Rm. 218
Missoula, MT 59801
(406) 543-7606*
9:00 AM–6:00 PM

Nebraska

**Rape/Spouse Abuse
Crisis Center**
1133 H. St.
Lincoln, NE 68508
(402) 475-7273*

Women Against Violence
YWCA
3929 Harney St., Rm. 100
Omaha, NE 68131
(402) 345-7273*
9:00 AM–5:00 PM

Nevada

**Community Action
Against Rape**
749 Veterans Memorial Dr.,
Room 79
Las Vegas, NV 89101
(702) 735-7111 *(hotline)*
(702) 385-2153 *(office)*

New Hampshire

Women's Crisis Line for Rape Victims and Battered Women
YWCA
72 Concord St.
Manchester, NH 03101
(603) 668-2299 *(hotline)*
(603) 625-5785 *(office)*

Rape and Assault Committee for the Nashua Area, Inc.
10 Prospect St., P.O. Box 217
Nashua, NH 03061
(603) 883-3044 *(hotline)*
(603) 889-5762 *(office)*

New Jersey

Rape Program Crisis Intervention Unit
East Orange General Hospital
300 Central Ave.
East Orange, NJ 07019
(201) 672-9685*

Sexual Assault Rape Analysis Unit (S.A.R.A.)
22 Franklin St.
Newark, NJ 07102
(201) 733-7273*
9:00 AM–2:00 AM

New Mexico

Albuquerque Rape Crisis Center
905 Vassar, N.E.
Albuquerque, NM 87106
(505) 247-0707 *(hotline)*
(505) 242-4619 *(office)*
8:00 AM–5:00 PM

Santa Fe Rape Crisis Center, Inc.
Box 2822
Santa Fe, NM 87501
(505) 982-4667*
8:30 AM–5:00 PM

Community Against Rape, Inc.
Box 3170
Taos, NM 87571
(505) 758-2910*

New York

Borough Crisis Center Mayor's Task Force on Rape
Lincoln Hospital
234 E. 149th St.
Bronx, NY 10451
(212) 579-5326, 579-5327,
or 579-5328*

Anti-Rape Advocacy
Crisis Services, Inc.
3258 Main St.
Buffalo, NY 14214
(716) 834-3131*

Rape Intervention Program
St. Luke's/Roosevelt
Hospital Center
44 Morningside Dr., #1
New York, NY 10025
(212) 870-1875 or 870-1048
24-hour services

Rape Crisis Program
Department of Community
Medicine
St. Vincent's Hospital
153 W. 11th St.
New York, NY 10011
(212) 790-8068
(212) 790-8000 (evenings, weekends)
9:00 AM–5:00 PM
24-hour services

Rape Crisis Service of Planned Parenthood of Rochester and Monroe County
24 Windsor St.
Rochester, NY 14605
(716) 546-2595*

101

Rape Crisis Center of Syracuse, Inc.
423 W. Onandaga St.
Syracuse, NY 13202
(315) 422-7273*
8:30 AM–5:00 PM

North Carolina

Chapel Hill—Carrboro Rape Crisis Center
Box 871
Chapel Hill, NC 27514
(919) 967-7273 (hotline)
(919) 929-0471, ext 240
(office)
10:00 AM–2:00 PM

Charlotte-Mecklenburg Rape Crisis Service
P.O. Box 29055
Charlotte, NC 28212
(704) 373-0982*

Rape Crisis Center of Raleigh
401 E. Whitiker Mill Rd.
Raleigh, NC 27650
(919) 755-6661*

North Dakota

Rape and Abuse Crisis Center of Fargo-Moorhead
P.O. Box 1655
Fargo, ND 58107
(701) 293-7273*

Grand Forks Rape Crisis Center
319 S. Sixth
Grand Forks, ND 58201
(701) 746-8900 (hotline)

Ohio

Akron Rape Crisis Center
St. Paul's Episcopal Church
146 High St.
Akron, OH 44308
(216) 434-7273*

**Women Helping
Women, Inc.**
216 E. 9th St.
Cincinnati, OH 45202
(513) 381-5610 (hotline)
(513) 381-6003 (office)

**Toledo United Against
Rape**
108 Eaglepoint Rd.
Rossford, OH 43460
(419) 885-5787*

**Community Guidance
and Human Services
Mental Health Center**
3740 Euclid
Cleveland, OH 44115
(216) 431-7774
8:30 AM–5:00 PM Mon–
Wed, Fri
8:30 AM–9:00 PM Thurs
24-hour services

Women Against Rape
P.O. Box 02084
Columbus, OH 43202
(614) 221-4447 *(hotline)*
(614) 291-9751 *(information)*

Oklahoma

**YWCA Women's Resource
Center—Rape Crisis**
135 N.W. 19th
Oklahoma City, OK 73118
(405) 524-7273 *(hotline)*
(405) 528-5440 *(office)*
9:00 AM–5:00 PM

Women's Resource Center
P.O. Box 5089
Norman, OK 73071
(405) 364-9424*
8:00 AM–5:00 PM Mon–Fri

Oregon

Rape Crisis Center
P.O. Box 914
216 S.W. Madison,
Corvallis, OR 97330
(503) 754-0110*

Women's Crisis Service
P.O. Box 851
Salem, OR 97308
(503) 399-7722 (hotline)
(503) 378-1572 (office)

Rape Victim Advocate Project
Multnomah County District
Attorney
804 Multnomah County
Courthouse
Portland, OR 97204
(503) 248-5059
24-hour services

Pennsylvania

Rape Crisis Council of Lehigh Valley, Inc.
P.O. Box 1445
Allentown, PA 18105
(215) 437-6610
or 437-6611*

Women Organized Against Rape
1220 Sansom St.
Philadelphia, PA 19107
(215) 922-3434 (hotline)
(215) 922-7400 (office)
9:00 AM–5:00 PM

Erie County Rape Crisis Center
4518 Peach St.
Erie, PA 16503
(814) 868-0314*

Pittsburgh Action Against Rape
211 S. Oakland Ave.
Pittsburgh, PA 15213
(412) 765-2731 *(hotline)*
(412) 682-0219 *(office)*

Women's Center and Shelter of Greater Pittsburgh
P.O. Box 5147
Pittsburgh, PA 15206
(412) 661-6066*

Women's Resource Center
Chamber of Commerce Bldg.
Scranton, PA 18503
(717) 346-4671*

Rape Counseling Information Service of Fayette County, Inc.
62 E. Church St.
Uniontown, PA 15401
(412) 437-3737 *(hotline)*
(412) 437-3738 *(office)*

Puerto Rico

Centro De Ayuda a Victimas de Violacion
Apartado CH-11321, Caparra Heights Station
Caparra Heights, PR 00922
(809) 765-2285 *(hotline)*
(809) 765-2412 *(office)*

Cayey Mental Health Center
392 Jose De Diego Ave. West
Cayey, PR 00633
(809) 738-5049, 738-5020, or 738-2222
24-hour services

Rhode Island

Newport County Community Mental Health Center, Inc.
65 Valley Rd.
Middletown, RI 02840
(401) 846-1213*

Rhode Island Rape Crisis Center, Inc.
235 Promenade St., Rm. 202
Providence, RI 02908
(401) 941-2400
on call 24 hours

South Carolina

People Against Rape
150 Meeting St.
Charleston, SC 29401
(803) 722-7273*

Rape Crisis Council of Greenwood
Beckman Center P.O. Drawer 70
Greenwood, SC 29646
(800) 223-4357 *(hotline)*
(803) 223-8331 *(Beckman Ctr.)*

South Dakota

Aberdeen Area Rape Task Force
317 S. Kline
Aberdeen, SD 57401
(605) 226-1212*
1:00–9:00 PM Mon–Sat

Rape Education, Advocacy and Counseling Team (REACT)
Brookings Women's Center
802 11th Ave.
Brookings, SD 57006
(605) 688-4518*
or emergency 911 *(police)*

Tennessee

Rape and Sexual Abuse Center of Davidson County
1908 21st Ave. South
Nashville, TN 37212
Mailing address:
P.O. Box 120831
Nashville, TN 37212
(615) 327-1110*

Knoxville Rape Crisis Center
P.O. Box 2262
Knoxville, TN 37901
(615) 522-7273 *(hotline)*
(615) 522-4745 *(office)*

Rape Crisis and Sexual Abuse Service
804 S. Bryan, Suite 207
Amarillo, TX 79106
(806) 373-8022*
9:00 AM–5:00 PM

Dallas County Rape Crisis Center
P.O. Box 35728
Dallas, TX 75235
(214) 521-1020*

Rape Crisis Services
El Paso Mental Health/Mental Retardation
5308 El Paso Dr.
El Paso, TX 79905
(915) 779-1800 (hotline)
(915) 779-7383 (office)

Rape Crisis Support of Tarrant County
1203 Lake St., #208
Forth Worth, TX 76102
(817) 335-7273*

People Against Rape/Abuse, Inc. (PARA)
P.O. Box 57535
Houston, TX 77598
(713) 488-7222*

Waco Rape Crisis Center
P.O. Box 464,
1609 Austin Ave.
Waco, TX 76701
(817) 752-1113 *(hotline)*
(817) 752-9330 *(office)*

YWCA—Women's Crisis Shelter
505 27th St.
Ogden, UT 84403
(801) 392-7273 (hotline)
(801) 394-9456 (office)

Utah County Rape Crisis Line
P.O. Box 1375
Provo, UT 84601
(801) 226-8989*

Vermont

Women's Crisis Center
P.O. Box 933
Brattleboro, VT 05301
(802) 254-6954*

Women's Rape Crisis Center
P.O. Box 92
Burlington, VT 05401
(802) 863-1236*

Virginia

Fairfax County Victim Assistance Network
8119 Holland Rd.
Alexandria, VA 22306
(703) 360-7273 (hotline)
(703) 360-6910 (office)

YWCA Women's Victim Advocacy Program
6 N. 5th St.
Richmond, VA 23219
(804) 643-0888 *(hotline)*
(804) 643-6761 *(office)*

Charlottesville Rape Crisis Group
214 Rugby Rd.
Charlottesville, VA 22901
(804) 977-7273*

Washington

Alternatives to Violence
P.O. Box 2615, College Station
Pullman, WA 99163
(509) 332-4357*

Seattle Rape Relief
1825 S. Jackson, #102
Seattle, WA 98144
(206) 632-7273*

Whatcom County Rape Relief
Whatcom County Crisis Services
Mason Bldg, 124 E. Holly,
Rm. 201
Bellingham, WA 98225
(206) 676-1175 *(hotline)*
(206) 671-5754 *(office)*

Rape Crisis Network
N. 1226 Howard St.
Spokane, WA 99201
(509) 624-7273*
8:30 AM–5:00 PM

West Virginia

Sexual Assault Information Center, Inc.
1036 Quarrier St., #317
Charleston, WV 25301
(304) 344-9834 *(hotline)*
(304) 344-9839 *(office)*
9:00 AM–5:00 PM
24-hour services

Wisconsin

Green Bay Rape Crisis Center, Ltd.
131 S. Madison St.
Green Bay, WI 54301
(414) 433-0584*

Rape Crisis Center
312 E. Wilson St.
Madison, WI 53703
(608) 251-7273
10:00 AM–2:00 PM
(or by appointment)
24-hour advocate services

Women's Crisis Line
1428 N. Farwell Ave.
Milwaukee, WI 53202
(414) 964-7535 (hotline)
(414) 271-8112 (office)

Rape Crisis/Domestic Abuse Center
660 Oak St.
Oshkosh, WI 54901
(414) 233-7707 *(hotline)*
(414) 426-1460 *(office)*
24-hour services

Wyoming

Western Wyoming Mental Health Association
115 W. Snow King Ave,
P.O. Box 1868
Jackson, WY 83001
(307) 733-2046
(800) 442-6383 *(toll-free in-state number)*
24-hour emergency services

CANADA

Alberta

Calgary Rape Crisis Centre
202-723 14th St. N.W.
Calgary, Alberta, Canada

Rape Crisis Centre of Edmonton
416-10010-105 St.
Edmonton, Alberta,
Canada T5J 1C4
(403) 429-0023

British Columbia

Naniamo Rape Relief Centre
361 Vancouver Ave.
Naniamo, British Columbia,
Canada V9S 4G3
(604) 753-0022 (hotline)
(604) 753-1021 (office)

Victoria Rape/Assault Centre
1947 Cook St.
Victoria, British Columbia,
Canada
(604) 383-5545

Vancouver Anti-Sexual Assault Centre
4-45 Kingsway
Vancouver, British
Columbia,
Canada V5T 3H7
(604) 732-1613 (hotline)

Manitoba

**Rape Crisis and
Information
Centre (Klinic, Inc.)**
545 Broadway Ave.
Winnipeg, Manitoba,
Canada R3C 0W3
(204) 774-4525 *(hotline)*
(204) 786-6943 *(office)*

New Brunswick

**Fredericton Rape Crisis
Service**
P.O. Box 1033
Fredericton, New Brunswick,
Canada E3B 5C2
(506) 454-0437

**Moncton Anti-Sexual Assault
Centre**
Box 474
Moncton, New Brunswick,
Canada
(506) 388-4333

New foundland

**St. John's Rape Crisis
and Information Centre**
P.O. Box 6072
St. John's, Newfoundland,
Canada A1C 5X8
(709) 726-1411 *(hotline)*
(709) 753-0220 *(office)*

Ontario

**Hamilton Rape Crisis
Centre**
215 Main St.
Hamilton, Ontario, Canada
(416) 525-4573

Ottawa Rape Crisis Centre
P.O. Box 35, Station B
Ottawa, Ontario, Canada
(613) 238-6666 (hotline)
(613) 238-6667 (office)

**Algoma District Sexual
Assault Centre**
Box 785
Sault Ste. Marie, Ontario,
Canada
(705) 949-5200

Toronto Rape Crisis Centre
Box 6597, Postal Station A
Toronto, Ontario,
Canada M5W 1X4
(416) 964-8080 *(hotline)*
(416) 964-7477 *(office)*

**Sexual Assault Crisis
Centre of Essex County**
1598 Ouellette
Windsor, Ontario, Canada
(519) 253-3100

Quebec

**Hull Centre d'Aide aux
Victimes de Viol**
C.P. 1872, Succursale B
Hull, Quebec, Canada
(819) 771-1773

Montreal Women's Aid
C.P. 82, Station E
Montreal, Quebec, Canada
(514) 270-8291

**Mouvement contre le Viol
Collective de Montreal**
C.P. 391, Succursale Delormier
Montreal, Quebec, Canada
(514) 526-2460

Regina Women's Community Centre and Rape Crisis Line
1810 Smith St., Rm. 219
Regina, Saskatchewan,
Canada S4P 1X7
(306) 352-0434

Saskatoon Rape Crisis Centre
D249 2nd Ave. South
Saskatoon, Saskatchewan,
Canada

Appendix C

A Guide to Victim Assistance Programs in the United States

You can use this guide to help you locate victim services and compensation programs in your state. Contact these offices for assistance and for information concerning financial reimbursement for expenses you may have incurred as the survivor of a violent crime. Your local rape crisis center should also have information on compensation and assistance programs in your area. Finally, you can contact the National Organization for Victim Assistance (NOVA) at 1757 Park Road, N.W., Washington, DC 20010 (202) 232-8560, for further information.

Alabama

District Attorney's Office
142 Washington Ave., Suite 303
Montgomery, AL 36104
(205) 263-3816

Arkansas

Prosecuting Attorney's Office
Seb. City Court House, Rm. 301
Fort Smith, AR 72901
*(501) 783-8976

Alaska

Assistant Attorney General
Pouch KT
Juneau, AK 99811
(907) 465-3678
(907) 465-3040

California

California Victim/Witness Assistance Program
9719 Lincoln Village Drive
Sacramento, CA 95827
(916) 366-5437

Arizona

Maricopa County Attorney's Victim/Witness Program
101 W. Jefferson Ave., 4th Fl.
Phoenix, AZ 85003
(602) 262-8581

Colorado

Victim/Witness Assistance Unit
Office of the District Attorney
P.O. Box 471
Boulder, CO 80306
(303) 441-3730

Connecticut

Victim/Witness Program
Office of the State's Attorney
95 Washington St.
Hartford, CT 06106
(203) 566-3190

Florida

Victim/Witness Services
Office of the State Attorney
330 E. Bay St., Rm. 517
Jacksonville, FL 32202
(904) 633-6634

Delaware

**Department of Justice
Victim Service Unit**
State Office Building
820 French St.
Wilmington, DE 19801
(302) 571-2599

Georgia

**Victim/Witness
Assistance Program**
Solicitor's Office
P.O. Box 649
Marietta, GA 30061
(404) 429-3599

District of Columbia

**Office of Crime Victims
Compensation Program**
500 C St., N.W., Room #626
Washington, DC 20010
(202) 724-3930

Hawaii

**Office of the Prosecuting
Attorney**
Kauai County Victim/Witness
Program
4396 Rice St.
Lihue, HI 96766
(808) 245-9090

Idaho

Office of the Attorney General
State House
Boise, ID 83720
(208) 334-2400

Illinois

Crime Victims Program

Department of the Attorney General
22nd Floor, Suite 2200
188 West Randolph
Chicago, IL 60601
(312) 793-2585

Indiana

Victim Assistance Program
Ft. Wayne Police Department
City-County Building
Fort Wayne, IN 46802
(219) 423-7576

Iowa

State of Iowa Crime Victims Reparation Program
Department of Public Safety
Wallace Building
Des Moines, IA 50319
(515) 281-5044

Kansas

Kansas Office of the Attorney General
Judicial Center
Topeka, KS
(913) 296-2215

Kentucky

Victim Information Program
Commonwealth's Attorney's Office
315 Legal Arts Building
200 S. 7th St.
Louisville, KY 40202
(502) 581-5823

Louisiana

Victim/Witness Assistance Bureau

Office of the District Attorney
619 S. White St.
New Orleans, LA 70119
(504) 822-2414, ext. 553

Maine

Victim/Witness Services

Office of the District Attorney
97 Hammond St.
Bangor, ME 04401
(207) 945-9467

Maryland

Victim/Witness Unit Director

Baltimore City State's
Attorney's Office
Court House West, Rm. 410
Baltimore, MD 21201
(301) 396-1897

Massachusetts

Commonwealth of Massachusetts
Victim Compensation
Resource
Assistant Attorney General
Torts Division
One Ashburton Pl
Boston, MA 02108
(617) 727-5025

Michigan

Victim/Witness Services

Prosecuting Attorney's Office
227 W. Michigan Ave.
Kalamazoo, MI 49007
(616) 383-8677 or
(616) 383-8865

Minnesota

Victim/Witness Program

Government Center
300 S. 6th St., Rm. 2000
Minneapolis, MN 55487
(612) 348-5545

Mississippi

Harrison County Family Court
P.O. Box 7
Gulfport, MS 39501
(601) 863-9781

Missouri

Victim/Witness Assistance Unit
Municipal Court Bldg
1320 Market St., Rm. 330
St. Louis, MO 63103
(314) 622-4373

Montana

Crime Victims Unit
Worker's Compensation
Division
815 Front St.
Helena, MT 59601
(406) 499-5633

Nebraska

Victim/Witness Unit
Lincoln Police Department
233 S. 10th St.
Lincoln, NB 68508
(402) 471-7181

Nevada

Victim/Witness Assistance Center
Clark County District Attorney's
Office
300 S. Fourth St., Suite 1111
Las Vegas, NV 89101
(702) 386-4779

New Hampshire

Victim/Witness Assistance Unit
Hillsborough County District
Attorney's Office
300 Chestnut St.
Manchester, NH 03101
(603) 669-1053

New Jersey

**Violent Crimes
Compensation Board**
60 Park Place
Newark, NJ 07102
(201) 648-2107

North Carolina

**Assistant to the Attorney
General for Criminal
Justice Affairs**
Office of the Attorney General
P.O. Box 629
Raleigh, NC 27602
(919) 733-3377

New Mexico

**Crime Victims Reparations
Commission**
P.O. Box 871
Albuquerque, NM 87103
(505) 842-3904

North Dakota

Crime Victims Reparations
North Dakota Worker's
Compensation Bureau
Russell Bldg—Highway 83 N.
Bismark, ND 58501
(701) 224-2700

New York

**District Attorney Victim/
Witness Assistance Unit**
Public Safety and Judicial
Services
205 County Office Bldg
Rochester, NY 14614
(716) 428-5885

Ohio

Victim/Witness Program
Memorial Community Center
159 Dorchester Ave.
Cincinnati, OH 45210
(513) 621-7606

Oklahoma

Office of the Attorney General

State Capitol Building
Oklahoma City, OK 73105
(405) 521-3921

Rhode Island

Office of the Attorney General
72 Pine St.
Providence, RI 02903
(401) 274-4400

Oregon

Victims Assistance Program

Multnomah county District
Attorney's Office
1021 S.W. 4th—Rm. 804
Portland, OR 97204
(503) 248-3222

South Carolina

Victim/Witness Assistance
Greenville County
Courthouse, Rm. 318
Greenville, SC 29601
(803) 298-8647

Pennsylvania

Witness Assistance Unit

District Attorney's Office
2300 Centre Square West
Philadelphia, PA 19102
(215) 275-6199

South Dakota

Victim's Assistance Program
Court Services Dept., 7th
Judicial Circuit
703 Adams Rd.
Rapid City, SD 57701
(605) 394-2595

Tennessee

Victim/Witness Unit
Criminal Justice Center
201 Poplar Ave., Suite 301
Memphis, TN 38103
(901) 577-5946

Virginia

Victim/Witness Program
Commonwealth's Attorney's
Office
City of Portsmouth, P.O.
Box 1417
Portsmouth, VA 23705
(804) 393-8581

Texas

The Victim-Witness Office
201 Fannin, Rm. 200
Houston, TX 77002
(713) 221-6655

Washington

Victim Assistance Unit
King County Prosecutor
516 3rd Ave., King County
Courthouse
Seattle, WA 98104
(206) 583-2200

Utah

**The Victim/Witness
Counseling Unit**
Salt Lake County Attorney's
Office
460 S. 3rd E.
Salt Lake City, UT 84111
(801) 535-5558

West Virginia

17th Judicial Circuit
Monogalia County Court
House
Morgantown, WV 26505
(304) 291-7265

Wisconsin

Victim/Witness Services

Milwaukee County District
Attorney's Office
412 Safety Bldg.,
821 W. State St.
Milwaukee, WI 53233
(414) 278-4659

Wyoming

**State Office on Family
Violence/Sexual Assault**

Mathaway Bldg., #451
Cheyenne, WY 82002
(307) 777-6086

Index

About the Author

Herma Silverstein is a successful author of a number of books for teenagers, including *Teenage Depression, Alcoholism, Teenage and Pregnant: What You Can Do*, and *A Teen Guide to Single Parenting*. She has a special interest in problems facing today's young people and has taken graduate studies in psychology at UCLA. Ms. Silverstein is the mother of two sons and makes her home in the Los Angeles area.